Ludwig van Beethoven
(1770-1827)

Dances

Danses

Tänze

I

for piano • pour piano • für Klavier

Urtext

K 197

INDEX

12 Menuette, WoO 7

12 deutsche Tänze, WoO 8

6 Menuette, WoO 10

1.  34

2.  35

3.  36

4.  37

5.  38

6.  39

7 ländlerische Tänze, WoO 11

1.  40

2.  40

3.  41

4.  42

5.  42

6.  43

7.  43

12 deutsche Tänze, WoO 13

1. 

45

2.  46

3.  47

4.  48

5.  49

6.  50

7.  51

8.  52

9.  53

10.  54

11.  55

12.  56

9 Contredanses, WoO 14

1.  60

5.  63

2.  60

6. 

64

3.  62

7.  64

4.  62

8.  65

9.  65

6 ländlerische Tänze, WoO 15

1.  66

4.  67

2.  66

5.  68

3.  67

6.  68

Anglaise in D, Hess 61

 70

Allemande in A, WoO 81

71

Menuetto in Es, WoO 82

Moderato

 72

6 Ecossaises, WoO 83

1. 

74

2. 

74

3. 
74

4. 
75

5. 
75

6. 
75

Walzer in Es, WoO 84

76

Walzer in D, WoO 85

77

Ecossaise in Es, WoO 86

77

Polonaise in C, Op. 89

Alla Polacca, vivace

78

12 Menuette

WoO 7
1795

2.
p
ff
6
sf
12
Trio
17
22
27
Da Capo

3.
ff
6
sf
tr
11
sf
tr
Trio
17
p
22
27
Da Capo

4.
sf
p
ff
Trio
Da Capo

5.
f
sf
Trio
p
ff
Da Capo

6.
sf
tr
Trio
1.
2.
f
Da Capo

7.
Trio
Da Capo

8.
Trio
Da Capo

9.
Trio
Da Capo

10.
f
6
11
sf
tr
Trio
17
22
p Echo
27

33
38
f
sf
44
p
Echo
Da Capo
11.
sf
sf
sf
6
tr
fp
pp

12
ff
Trio
17
fp
tr
fp
22
f
sf
27
ff
fp
Da Capo

12.
Trio
Da Capo

12 deutsche Tänze

WoO 8
1795

1.

2.

Trio
17
dolce
25
sf
sf
Da Capo
3.
f
tr
tr
9
sf
sf
Trio
17
f
p
25
f
f
p
Da Capo

4.
Trio
Da Capo

5.
ff
6
11
sf
Trio
17
25
Da Capo

6.
f
p
9
ff
Trio
17
p
22
f
27
p
Da Capo

7.
p
ff
sf
Trio
f
Da Capo

8.
sf
Trio
f
p
ff
Da Capo

9.
sf
6
11
ff
Trio
17
p dolce
22
27
Da Capo

10.
Trio
Da Capo

11.
f
Trio
p
Da Capo

12.
Trio
Coda segue

Coda
ff
7
12
18
23
Posthorn
mf
30

38
tutti
f
44
50
56
p cresc.
62
f
68
Posthorn
p
tutti
ff
Posthorn
p

74
tutti
ff
Posthorn
p
tutti
ff
80
88
94
p
100
Posthorn
tutti
p

Posthorn
tutti
f
ff
Posthorn

6 Menuette

WoO 10
1795

2.
Trio
Da Capo

3.
Trio
Da Capo

4.
Trio
Da Capo

5.
ff
sf
6
11
Trio
17
fp
22
27
Da Capo

6.
Trio
Da Capo

7 ländlerische Tänze

WoO 11
1798

1.

2.

3.

4.

5.

6.

7.

Coda
sf
tr

12 deutsche Tänze

WoO 13
ca 1800

2.

3.
f
6
sf
sf
11
sf
sf
Trio
17
22
28
Da Capo

4.
sf
fp
Trio
Da Capo

5.
f
9
sf
sf
sf
Trio
17
dolce
23
29
35
Da Capo

6.
9
Trio
17
p
sf
22
27
Da Capo

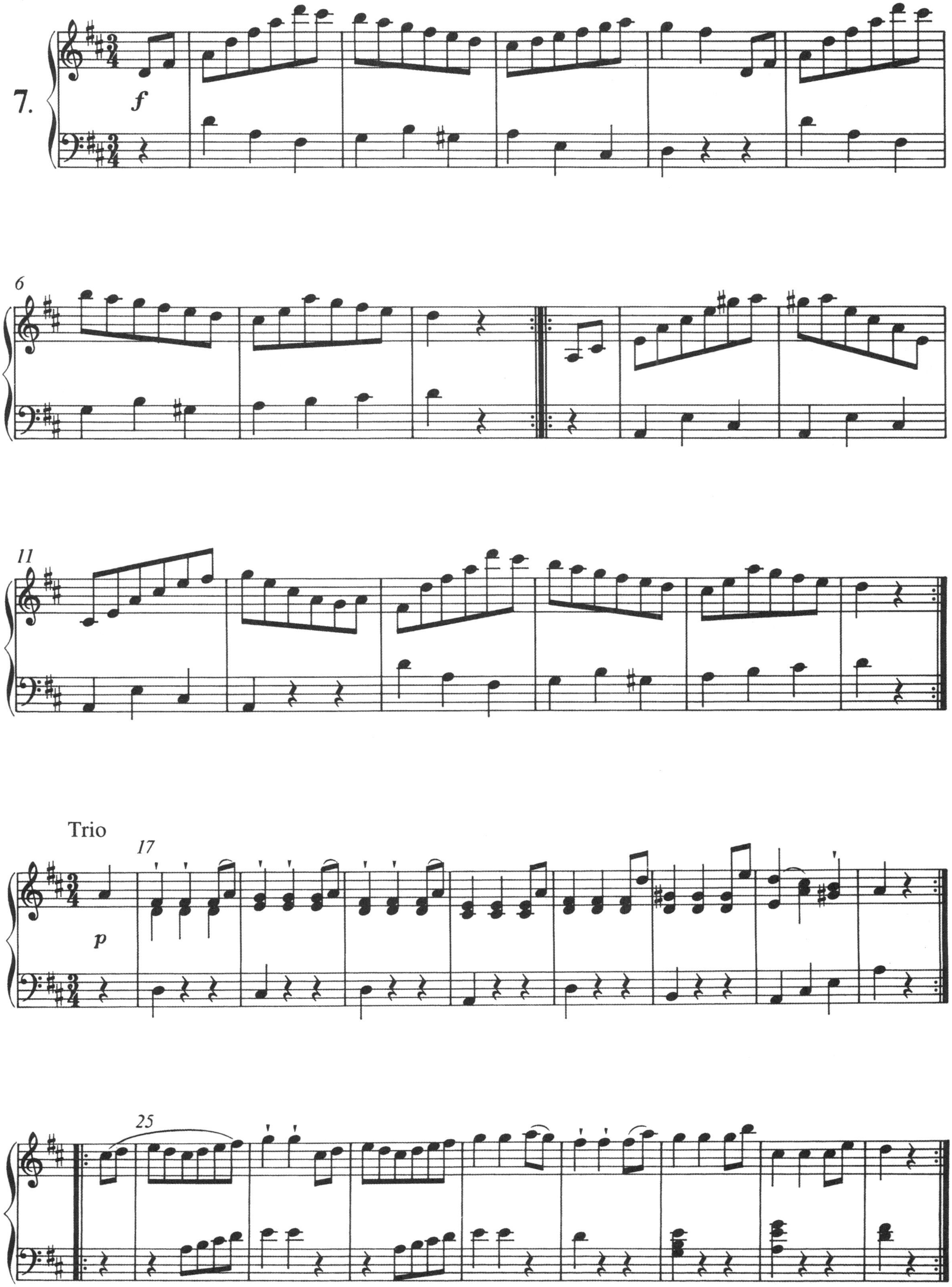
7.
f
6
11
Trio
17
p
25
Da Capo

Da Capo

K 197

9.
p
sf
sf
sf
9
Trio
17
22
27
Da Capo

Da Capo

11.
7
f
12
1.
2.
Trio
17
ff
p
25
ff
p
Da Capo

12.
ff
sf
5
11
Trio
17
p
25
attacca subito la Coda

Coda

29
35
41
ff
47
53
f

59
f
f
65
ff
sf
71
sf
sf
1.
2.
sf
76
sf
83
ff

9 Contredanses

WoO 14
1800-1801

11
Segue Trio
Trio
17
22
29
35
No. 2 Da Capo

3.
Segue Trio
Trio
No. 3 Da Capo
4.

Segue Trio
Trio
cresc.
No. 4. Da Capo
5.

6.
sempre p
5
11
Segue No. 7
7.
cresc.
6
11

8.
p
sf
p
6
f
12
sf
p
f
Segue No. 9
9.
p
6
1.
2.
f
11

6 ländlerische Tänze

WoO 15
1802

3.

4.

5.
sf
6
11
6.

11
Coda
7
13
20

Anglaise in D

Hess 61
ca 1800

Allemande in A

WoO 81
ca 1800

[*Da Capo*]

Menuetto in Es

WoO 82
ca 1803

Trio
Men. Da Capo

6 Ecossaises

WoO 83
ca 1806

9
f
Dal 𝄋 al 𝄌
4.
Dal 𝄋 al 𝄌
5.
9
Dal 𝄋 al 𝄌
6.
9
Dal 𝄋 al 𝄌

Walzer in Es

WoO 84
1824

Walzer in D

WoO 85
1825

Ecossaise in Es

WoO 86
1825

A S.M. Elisabetha Alexiewna imperatrice de toutes les Russies

Polonaise in C

Op. 89
1814

8
dolce
tr
12
16
p
dim.
pp
20
pp
dolce
tr
24

28
cresc.
30
f
p
fp
f fp
33
36
f fp
39
f fp
fp

42
fp
dimin.
45
pp
f
fp
48
cresc.
f
51
tr
54
tr
58

62
p
dim.
pp
66
pp
tr
70
73
cresc.
76
f
p
p

80
cresc.
84
dim.
p
dolce
88
cresc.
92
p
cresc.
poco ritard.
96
dim.

a tempo
99
tr
102
tr
105
tr
cresc.
f
108
sf
111
114
dim.
p
6

117
cresc.
dim.
119
dolce
tr
123
cresc.
127
f
131
cresc.
p
135
tr
cresc.
f
p
Ped.

139
tr
142
cresc.
f
145
p
cresc.
148
151
6
3
5

154
p
157
p
p
Ped.
ossia:
(Beethoven)
tr
poco adagio
161
cresc.
cresc.
tr
p
tr
il primo tempo
166
pp
cresc. - - - - f

KÖNEMANN

www.koenemann.com

Editor: István Máriássy
Responsible co-editor: Tamás Záskaliczky
Technical editor: Dezső Varga
Engraved by Kottamester Bt., Budapest

ISBN 978-3-7419-1421-8

Printed in Spain by LitoStamp